THE LORD LOOSETH THE PRISONER

Frank Sherry

Printed in the United States of America

Scriptures quoted in this book are from the King James Version of the Bible

First Printing	1993	1,000 copies
Second Printing	1993	5,000 copies
Third Printing	1996	5,000 copies
Fourth Printing	1999	5,000 copies
Fifth Printing (revised)	2000	5,000 copies
Sixth Printing	2002	10,000 copies

"And they came over unto the other side of the sea, into the country of the Gadarenes.

And when he was come out of the ship, immediately there met him out of the tombs a man with an unclean spirit. Who had his dwelling among the tombs; and no man could bind him, no, not with chains.

Because that he had been often bound with fetters and chains, and the chains had been plucked asunder by him, and the fetters broken in pieces; neither could any man tame him.

And always night and day, he was in the mountains, and in the tombs, crying and cutting himself with stones. But when he saw Jesus afar off, he ran and worshipped him. And cried with a loud voice, and said, 'What have I to do with thee, Jesus, thou Son of the most high God? I adjure thee by God, that thou torment me not.' For he said unto him, 'Come out of the man, thou unclean spirit.'

And he asked him, 'What is thy name?' And he answered, saying, 'My name is Legion, for we are many.'

And he besought him much that he would not send them away out of the country.

Now there was nigh unto the mountains a great herd of swine feeding. And all the devils besought him; saying, 'Send us into the swine that we may enter into them.'

And forthwith Jesus gave them leave. And the unclean spirits went out, and entered into the swine: and the herd ran violently down a deep place into the sea, (there were about two thousand) and were choked in the sea.

And they that fed the swine fled, and told it in the city, and in the country. And they went out to see what it was that was done. And they came to Jesus, and seeing him that was possessed with the devil, and had the legion, sitting, and clothed, and in this right mind; and they were afraid.

And they that saw it told them how it befell to him that was possessed with the devil, and also concerning the swine. And they began to pray him to depart out of their coasts.

And when he was come into the ship, he that had been possessed with the devil prayed him that he might be with him. Howbeit, Jesus suffered him not, but saith unto him, 'Go home to thy friends, and tell them how great things the Lord hath done for thee, and hath had compassion on thee.'

And he departed, and began to publish in Decapolis how great things Jesus had done for him; and all men did marvel."

Mark 5: 1-20

Our wedding day, June 21, 1987 at Vienna Correctional Center with Jimmy Williams and Al Richardson

FORWARD

I have known many men who claimed conversion upon entering prison. Few of these conversions are real.

While warden at Menard Correctional Center in Chester, Illinois, I met Frank Sherry. Later, as warden of Vienna Correctional Center in Vienna, Illinois, we met again. During these times, I was able to witness his life; and observe the growth in his Christian walk.

While at Menard, Frank began to set aside time for prayer and the bible. He also encouraged others to do this. Frank witnessed of Christ and handed out tracts to the other residents.

Later at Vienna, he became part of a singing group. The group was given permission to sing and testify at local churches. As a Christian, I went along to these services; and did all I could to support and encourage their work for the Lord.

I can truthfully say, Frank was a positive influence at both centers. As a warden and a Christian, I know the hardships and problems he faced while in prison. He proved himself to be a true Christian. Upon his release, he has continued to work for the Lord.

Jim Greer

This book is dedicated to Florence Dace, a woman of great faith. She dared to face me while I was in the county jail with the love and forgiveness that is only possible through Jesus Christ our Lord. I killed her husband, but she said, "I must forgive you...and Jesus loves you."

(In the first printing of this story we did not use Florence's real name, even though she traveled with us to churches and never hid her identity. She went to be with the Lord in August of 1997.)

Frank Sherry and Florence Dace. Only God can give us the strength to forgive. He is a restorer.

STATE OF ILLINOIS

PRISONER REVIEW BOARD

Paul J. Klincar, Chairman

September 22, 1989

Mr. Francis H. Sherry
R. R. #1, Box 357
Marion, IL 62959

Re: Reg. No.: C-68067, Vienna
Ind. No.(s): 75-CF-357, 75-CF-354 (cs)
Crime(s): Vol. Manslaughter, Agg. Battery
Sent. Date(s): 03-17-76
County: Sangamon
Effective Date: September 20, 1989

Dear Mr. Sherry

You are hereby notified that you have been discharged from the above captioned sentence(s). This is in accordance with Illinois Revised Statutes, Chapter 38, Section 1003-3-8(b).

This letter is a certificate of release and discharge. Retain it with your legal records. A copy of this letter is being forwarded to the Circuit Clerk of the committing county and to the Department of Corrections.

Sincerely

Paul J. Klincar

Paul J. Klincar
Chairman

PJK:jde

cc: Circuit Clerk
Parole District - East St. Louis
Field Services
File
Superintendent

319 E. MADISON STREET, SUITE A / SPRINGFIELD, ILLINOIS 62701 / TELEPHONE (217) 782-7273

Chapter One

THE TORMENTORS

"Because that he had often been bound with fetters and chains, and the chains had been plucked asunder by him, and the fetters broken in pieces; neither could any man tame him." *Mark 5:4*

R-I-I-P!!!

The sound of velcro strips that held me bound to the table in the emergency room of the hospital added to my horror as I once again began to hallucinate. In the fog and delirium of my tortured soul, fear gripped me. Aliens, who earlier had ordered me to kill every living thing in my path, now had captured me and seemingly were biting and tearing at my flesh.

They were consuming me and the ghastly sounds terrorized my very soul.

Kill me! Kill me! I screamed. Unable to move, the tormentors continued to bind and gnaw at me. As I drifted

in and out of my drugged stupor, I saw a police officer hovering over me. He said, "I'd like to kill you."

"What happened? Where am I?" I cried, hours later in the hospital room. I didn't realize it, but I would have many years to ponder these questions and recall the events that led up to that fateful day of August 4, 1975.

The devil had been writing the script of my life since early childhood and now one man was dead and seven others were brutally beaten.

I began to seriously contemplate what life was all about and if life really mattered at all. My life had no significance, and now what life I had rolled to a screeching halt.

Sex, drugs and rock and roll had been my life, and it had led me down a dead end street to hell.

Despair and dread were waiting for me at the end of that street. What was life all about anyway? My philosophy had been to "do my own thing"--but now, violence and murder--what happened?

Chapter Two

INFERIORITIES

"When I was a child, I spake as a child, I understood as a child, I thought as a child; but when I became a man, I put away childish things." I Corinthians 13:11

Life as a young boy can be tough.

My father was in the Coast Guard and we lived in more states than I can remember. Just when I established a meaningful friendship, we would move and relocate in another state and I would have to find new friends. It wasn't easy because new kids are not always received with open arms in the government housing and new school systems.

Before the age of ten, I was sexually molested. This became a plague that hovered over me and would oppress me during the years to come. It would lead me to a promiscuous lifestyle to prove I was a man.

I learned to fight at an early age and that, I thought, helped me gain some respect. With all of our moving, I did a lot of fighting. I grew up with my share of inferiority complexes. At one point, I felt I was the skinniest boy in my school district. I thought that acne and pimples were going to overcome me during my adolescence. These complexes helped mold a fear of rejection into my soul and spirit that caused me to do daring and foolish stunts to gain attention.

One such incident opened the door for a life revolved around stealing. We lived in Groton, Connecticut and an older boy introduced me to the fine art of stealing. I didn't know what to steal, but he assured me that it didn't matter, that stealing anything would qualify me as a bonafide thief. On the momentous day of my initiation, I stole a can of wood putty. I felt I had a secret weapon to combat my fear of rejection and the complexes that hampered my school work and social behavior among my classmates. I began to steal from my classmates and break into schools as a means of lashing back. Stealing was to become a major bondage in my life, even at a young age. The compulsion to steal dominated the thinking of this young boy.

Shoplifting was a way of life. I remember the time when we were living in Fairfax, Virginia. I stole Christmas presents from the Post Exchange for my family. The police were investigating a theft ring in the nearby trailer park. I had a paper route there but I was not the thief. They summoned my parents and I to the police station to question me concerning the burglaries in the park. In fear of reprisal and a jail sentence I confessed everything I had ever stolen and promised not to steal again. Needless to say, I didn't keep my vow.

Chapter Three

MORMONISM

"O Lord our God, other lords beside thee, have had dominion over us; but by thee only will we make mention of your name." **Isaiah 26:13**

Life in the Sherry household revolved around the Mormon Church.

We were very involved and faithful. The people were friendly and it seemed like a nice environment to be a part of. I don't remember much about the church in my early years, but as I grew into my teens, I do remember a lot.

There are many programs in the Mormon Church to occupy one's time, and I was interested and participated. One program entailed three years of seminary training and indoctrination, which I completed. I attended these classes every morning before high school classes began. The church was attempting to groom me for a two year missionary venture and ultimately for the Melchizedek Priesthood, which is the highest order of the Mormon Church.

I trained quite extensively in the Mormon doctrine and studied for the "Priesthood". The church expected this diligence out of its young men. However, the girls seemed to take precedence, as far as I was concerned.

Girls were more important to me and this frustrated the Stake Bishop and the Elders. My heart wasn't in the church, its programs, or its activities.

I was told that when I received "a fire or a burning in my bosom" that I would truly become a convert and ready for the Lord's work.

The only fire I experienced was one of lust, and my heart wasn't interested in converting the masses of the world into Mormonism.

My obsession, at the time, was girls. Many times I was called into the Bishop's office to receive one of his "get serious" orations.

Testimony meetings were a joke. I avoided standing up and "sharing my testimony" because I didn't have one. When these meetings would start, I felt like slithering under the pew, then, a sharp elbow blow in my rib cage from my mother would indicate it was my turn to share my testimony. This signaled my recall and I shared how I was so happy to be a Mormon.

The Mormon hierarchy caught on to the fact that girls had dominion over me, and went so far as to have my steady girlfriend's membership transferred to another

Mormon church in the Dallas area. I was told this would make me regain my senses and recapture my vision to convert the world. Needless to say, this strategy didn't phase me. I began dating my steady girlfriend's best friend.

Music was becoming a predominant factor in my life.

The Beatles were acclaimed and I was fascinated with the lyrics and the "messages portrayed." This was the beginning of the hard rock era and I thrived on it.

As my senior year was coming to a close in 1967, a lot was going on in the Sherry household. Mom and Dad were having serious marital problems; my two sisters were young and I was in a world of my own. My older brother, Ross, had joined the Air Force several years earlier. The marital difficulties worsened, but were hidden from my sisters and me.

My own insecurities deepened with one complex after another.

I had big ears and was too skinny. An aptitude test revealed that I was not mechanically inclined.

Fears mounted in my life.

After my senior year, Mom and Dad divorced and

life became chaotic. It was hard on my sisters. Michelle, I later learned, had started drinking over at a friend's house and was sneaking out of the house after Mom thought she was in bed. After the divorce, at age 16, she ended up experimenting with LSD, marijuana, THC, and speed, together with drinking. She became pregnant the following year and attempted settling down and getting married.

I got a job working in a bomb factory in Garland, Texas. Life was miserable. Mom suggested that I join the Navy.

I tried enrolling in a junior college in the Dallas area, but my habitual thievery ended that endeavor.

I stole a credit card from a purse in one of the classrooms. When I attempted to use the credit card, the clerk wrote down my license number. I tried to return the credit card with many apologies, but the victim turned me into the security division of the college. Since I had virtually a clean record, I got my wrists slapped and was not arrested.

However, the administration did ask me to withdraw from school.

Chapter Four

IN THE NAVY

"The way of a fool is right in his own eyes; but he that hearkeneth to counsel is wise." **Proverbs 12:15**

"Why don't you join the Navy and make something out of your life?" queried my mom.

Mom had a way of getting a message across. I decided to take her advice. My tour in the United States Navy began in June 1968. After graduating from Great Lakes Naval Training Center, I was assigned to VF-121 Naval Air Station, Miramar, California. My introduction to drugs took place on my first day in my new squadron. My new friends and I took amphetamines, commonly known as "speed" or "crosstops" and had "rap sessions" for kicks. It seemed like we could solve any type of problem during these philosophical discussions. The adrenaline kick seemed to induce insight and revelation to a young man who had not previously indulged in drugs.

We remained under the influence of speed for days, and I was content.

The road to drug addiction began at this time. The flow of adrenaline was exciting and it seemed as if we could stay energized for days. The fact was that we did maintain these "runs" for days and only marijuana combined with beer could stabilize the effects. It seemed as if we were having more fun than anyone and that we were on top of the world.

The Navy supplied training films showing the horrors of heroin addiction. I prided myself in the fact that I would never get hooked on heroin--no way. Many of the enlisted men in my squadron were dopers. In this circle of friends, I found something that I had longed for all of my life: acceptance. The dopers or "heads", as they were known, wore leather wrist bands to distinguish themselves. We trusted one another and a strong rapport was established among the "heads".

Disdain and disrespect for authority began to take root and I did my own thing.

This was a training squadron for young pilots and we began to formulate a plan. We plotted to spike the officers coffee in the canteen with LSD. We never pulled it off for some reason, however, the seriousness or consequences of such a scheme were never considered.

My thievery escalated and I ripped off lockers, flight jackets, or anything that was accessible. One time I drove off base with a floor buffer in my back seat. I knew a bartender who needed one and I had no problem accommodating him.

My compulsion to steal dominated my thinking. This obsession drove me day after day. My eyes constantly searched for something of value that could be converted to cash. Little did I know that a silly can of wood putty would open the door to a bondage that would become a major stronghold to be reckoned with.

One of my favorite tricks was engineered on assignments in the barracks. We would be given duty to watch the barracks and keep them secure. As men came into the barracks, I would escort them to their cubicles and shine my flashlight on their combination locks so they could get into their lockers while making a mental note of the combination for my own later use. This caper worked well my entire four year enlistment.

We also had assignments from time to time for post watches. Our pilots were training in Phantoms and Crusaders. We would be assigned to the flight lines to guard these huge state of the art multi-million dollar aircraft's. What does that matter to a pothead? Very little. I would get high, go out on the flight lines and trip out on all of the brilliant hues and arrays of blue, red and green. When I came down somewhat from my high, I would crawl up into one of the huge intakes and take a nap. I did this on numerous occasions and had myself trained to awake at the slightest sound, especially if the officer of the deck was making rounds.

I met a young lady in the Enlisted Men's Club during my second year in the Navy. We hit it off and later married. She had a good job at a Title Insurance Company in San Diego. We lived in a small apartment off base and did well. Although we had no financial worries, we squandered our money on booze and drugs.

The parties were wild and I was getting deep into the hallucinogenic drugs.

We commonly tripped out on mescaline, THC, PCP and LSD. These are all mind altering drugs and induce hallucinations. The euphoria was unparalleled and pot and speed couldn't touch the "high" that the hallucinogens produced.

By my third year in the Navy, I had been busted three times for possession of marijuana. These infractions ensured me that a tour on an aircraft carrier was out of the question. My enlistment would run its course at Miramar; or so I thought.

My marriage never jelled. Constant drug use created an environment of suspicion, and my obsession with hallucinogens deepened this mistrust. Although we both abused alcohol and various stimulants and depressants, my wife abhorred my preoccupation with hallucinogens. This

was a constant barb in our marriage. Conflicts and arguments followed, with no hope for reconciliation. Life was souring, as it always had.

My last six months in the Navy cost me dearly. I was busted in the Post Exchange for "sales and transfer of a controlled substance." The substance was LSD. This was a first for our squadron. Many had been caught with pot, but no one had ever been caught distributing a controlled substance of this magnitude. I was assured by my Commanding Officer that this was a case of precedence and I was going to be made an example of intolerance to drug trafficking. Subsequently, I was court martialed and sentenced to six months hard labor, with a reduction to E-1 status, and a Bad Conduct Discharge.

This did not dampen my spirit however. My disdain and utter reproach for authority had hit its peak. All I wanted was my discharge from the Navy so I could do my thing. I despised authority and I despised our nation. As my brig time was nearing completion, I once again was confronted with a representative of the system I so vehemently opposed. He urged me to give the Navy one more year and promised an honorable discharge would await me if I kept my nose clean. I laughed at the audacity of such a proposal. I demanded my release and discharge. Drug addiction had really enlightened my mind.

Upon my discharge, my wife came to the base and picked me up. Something was different though. Something was awry. I had already managed to get high on some black

hash, but I could still discern that something had happened while I was away. As my wife and I drove south to San Diego I pondered the future of our marriage. It looked bleak at best. It was another man...and I knew him well. He was a mutual friend of ours. My wife and I were becoming estranged and had different agendas. It was convenient though, as I now felt justified to greater drunken and drug induced binges and greener pastures. I was liberated.

I was out of the Navy and could do my own thing.

Chapter Five

ON MY OWN

"There is a way that seemeth right to a man, but the end thereof are the ways of death." Proverbs 14:12

"Sex, drugs, and rock and roll" became my anthem as my partners and I raised hell in the San Diego area.

Our pool team in the neighborhood bar was called the "Reefers." We partied every night. One particular night that stands out vividly in my mind was a night that someone had scored some "window pane" LSD. This was potent and would mix well with some mescaline that I had. Mescaline is a derivative of the buttons in the peyote plant. The combination of LSD and mescaline would guarantee a powerful and excellent evening.

My wife and I hadn't separated yet, but it was just a matter of time. Mutual mistrust and suspicion permeated our home. That evening we were sitting around the house tripping on acid and mescaline. I was off like a jack rabbit. The combination of the drugs produced a dangerously powerful hallucinogenic effect.

One of my partners, Stan, a "crazy" like me, came over to the house. He wasn't high, but convinced me to drop another hit of acid with him so we could trip together. I knew better.

As high as I was, I could easily overdose and have a "bad trip", or even worse, kill myself.

Stan was convincing and I conceded to his chiding's and took another hit of acid. My wife had gone into the bedroom to get ready to go to the corner bar. Stan went into the bathroom. I suspected, in my hallucinations, that Stan was messing around with my wife. When he came into the living room, I jumped him and punched him several times. Realizing I was having a bad trip, he exited quickly, fearing for his life. I went into the bedroom to confront my unfaithful wife. She was high and became terrified as I screamed and yelled at her. I slapped her and cursed her several times and left the house.

The club we frequented was crowded and I stormed into the place higher than I had ever been. No one could deal with me and I was ordered to leave.

I crossed the street and literally terrorized the owner of a small store with my ravings. Inevitably, the police arrived. To this day, I don't understand why I wasn't arrested and taken into custody. Maybe the officers recognized me as one of the local misfits, and that I didn't

really mean to cause any trouble. Maybe they thought I was crazy. At any rate, I convinced the officers that I owned two blocks of the real estate they were standing on, and I wanted them to take me home. I told them I was a millionaire and could buy or sell them.

The officers took me home.

My buddy Stan came back to the house to see how I was. His face was full of stitches and he was a grinning mess. He had "tripped" up to the hospital and back, telling me how the emergency room produced a great psychedelic show for him. My wife would never return. Shortly after this incident, I threatened to throw her off the cliffs at Black's Beach in La Jolla. Trip after trip and high after high, I was digging a hole that was ensnaring me.

A burglary almost caused me to get shot. Even the San Diego County Jail seemed exciting to me. The felons and criminals were like heroes to me. The judge had mercy on me and I received a one year suspended sentence. My world was sinking deeper and deeper into a morass of darkness and hopelessness.

I moved in with a girl I knew from a local tavern. I stole her money and her dope. In her desperation she called one of her friends to handle the situation. Leaping into the living room, this man shot at me from two feet away. He aimed at my groin, but the bullet lodged in the chair between my legs. I jumped up, surprising him, and he

bolted away. Chasing him with a buck knife proved futile. His fear of reprisal probably saved my life; or serious injury. The same week an enraged drug dealer pulled a gun and knife on me to settle a score. Again and again my life was spared.

Life was reduced to living in a camper shell in someone's front yard. I was a vagrant. One morning, the owner of the house came out and adamantly told me to get out of his yard and threatened to call the police. Most of my so called friends now avoided me because I couldn't be trusted. I almost got killed many times as a result of stealing. I was at wits end with no hope.

I realized this lifestyle was going to get me killed, but didn't know the solution to my dilemma. I decided to go home to Carlinville, Illinois. I needed a change of pace and a roof over my head. I thought a change of scenery would cause a positive breakthrough in my life. I needed help. Mom would help me, and the change of environment would erase the past failures and disappointments. I would break out of this decline and turn my failures into success.

Carlinville, I had been told, was at one time designated to be the state capital, but the necessary funds were misappropriated. It is a small town with a population of 10,000. It never changed much--farmers, cornfields, barns, tractors and more cornfields. The land is flat and quite unlike the mass of freeways and skyscrapers in California. It was a humorous environment to this city boy fresh from the West Coast. Tractors drive slowly down the

streets and blacktop's and wizened old farmers sit around the feed stores and the public square.

I arrived in this big metropolis in 1973. I was twenty three years old. Most of my family lived in Carlinville and central Illinois, so my return seemed like a wise resolution.

I had been away from my family for so long that my return was somewhat awkward initially. Two slight obstacles confronted me: my family was not aware of my drug dependency nor my dishonorable discharge. I felt like the prodigal son returning home...

The Macoupin County Jail appeared to have been in existence eternally, and I soon discovered how its interior was decorated.

Michelle was married. She was still using drugs, but marriage and having two babies to care for enlightened her and she slowed down on partying.

My older brother was in the area and doing well. My youngest sister, Maureen, still lived with Mom. She was only twelve but already involved in drinking and stealing.

I had a cousin that I avoided. She was a fanatical Christian and bugged me about getting saved. She narrated a story about Jesus and the importance of becoming "born again."

Life in Carlinville turned out to be no different than life anywhere else. My mom and step-father were good to me, but I abused my privileges. They liked to drink and we did have that as a common denominator.

I quickly identified the local potheads and pill

poppers. They were everywhere. Later, as I reflected on Carlinville, it astounded me that such a small, country town could have the majority of its younger population on drugs. Michelle told me she didn't know anyone that wasn't using drugs. The "townies", as they were called, were a close knit group but could relate to another doper from California. Everyone I met was either smoking pot, popping pills, or tripping out on hallucinogens or pharmaceuticals. Drugs shipped from Southern California via the US mail service were no problem. The transition from freeway flyer to midwestern corn belt seemed to be a success.

Unknown to me, I was addicted to the illegal drugs I craved. I was also on the needle and had learned a long time ago that the intravenous method was the rapid technique to get the drugs into my system. In many drug circles this manner of obtaining a high is taboo and avoided. There were, however, several who "fired" up in Carlinville.

Syringes were not the easiest drug paraphernalia to acquire. My little niece was an insulin dependent diabetic, thus Michelle always had syringes in her possession. This, I reasoned, was a quick avenue to get my hands on the dangerous, unlawful paraphernalia. I implored Michelle to give me a syringe on two instances. The first time she hesitantly gave me one. The second and last time she gave me a syringe, she staunchly commanded me to never ask again.

I burglarized homes and fellow drug dealers just to get my hands on a syringe. I was a man driven with an obsession and mind fixation to get high--daily. Mainlining drugs into my system was the chief objective and became a methodical part of my daily routine.

I obtained different jobs, but could not keep one. Drugs and alcohol were too powerful a force and had dominated my life. I lost every job I had and wrecked every vehicle I drove, whether mine, borrowed or stolen. I recall wrecking or demolishing a total of twenty cars and trucks. It's conceivable there were accidents I have no recollection of. Typically, I drove on an invalid, suspended driver's license.

One of my arrests saved my life. I had been drinking and partying in the country and my buddies left me out in a field to walk to town. Staggering down the blacktop, I somehow made it to the edge of town and passed out in the middle of Locust Street. I was arrested for public drunkenness. Another incident involved a drunken binge that caused a tavern owner to call the police. I was waving a bag of dope around and behaving like a deranged lunatic. In my stupor, I was alerted of my imminent danger and managed to stash the dope in the back of the tavern. I was arrested and hauled to jail. As I was escorted in, I smashed my fist into a steel door. The man who left me in the country just happened to be in the bull pen. He cringed as he saw the California madman coming toward him. I was too dazed and confused to put two and two together and passed out on the steel bunk. He was relieved.

It was not unusual to see Mom and my step-father

raising hell at one of the local pubs they often frequented. Sometimes my brother, Ross, would be there too. We were such a happy family. In certain situations when the whole family was indulging, my mom would initiate the trouble. It was usually with the biggest, ugliest truck driver in the establishment. I wanted to sneak out the back door during these melees, but moms do need protection. One such tavern eighty-sixed us (kicked us out) for life.

When it became apparent to my Mom and step-father that Frank Sherry was not going to get his act together, they began to formulate a plan of action. Mom suggested that I go to Springfield, Illinois and look for work. I had worn out my welcome at home and the police department and judicial officials were tired of my repeated drunken sprees and disorderly conduct. One of the circuit judges threatened sentencing me to some time in a state prison.

Springfield sounded good. The seed was planted, a change was in order. The people there surely would appreciate me. I needed some fresh air and Carlinville had become stale and stagnant.

I still believed the illusion that changing my environment would resolve my problems.

Chapter Six

SPRINGFIELD, ILLINOIS

"It is as sport to a fool to do mischief; but a man of understanding has wisdom." **Proverbs 10:23**

Springfield, Illinois is the state capital. It also is much larger in population than the small town of Carlinville. I believed that the change would be good for me. Mom helped me get an apartment and my girlfriend moved in with me. She was a graduate of Blackburn College in Carlinville. She had a good job with the EPA. I managed to find some part-time work with a small construction crew. It seemed as if the change of pace had a settling effect on me.

There is an old adage, "birds of a feather flock together." It didn't take long to discover that my next door neighbor was a drug addict and needle freak. We became friends and shot up together at least twice daily. He introduced me to other users. These folks were on the ball. We frequented the taverns that catered to our type. The taverns did not actually approve of our activities, they simply looked the other way when transactions were going

down. They appreciated the money that was being spent in their joints. Their customers basically had the same agenda and they always had a pocketful of money.

I was "fixing" every day and all of my friends were on the needle. I would shoot anything into my arms from Barcardi Rum to LSD. Life revolved around daily fixes. I was physically, mentally, and psychologically addicted to barbiturates and pain killers. I abused any available drug that was on the streets.

My mind was shattered and I rapidly lost perception of reality. I had great difficulty locating my car, or even remembering whose car I had been driving, the day after a party.

Repeatedly I would have to remind myself that I had taken drugs and that was the reason for my disassociation and confusion with reality.

One such occasion occurred late one night driving home from Riverton, Illinois. I got lost and drove my Mercury into a tree. I then pulled into a farmer's lane. I don't remember the wreck or pulling into his lane. Ferocious dogs were barking and I envisioned that I was in a situation like "Mission Impossible". It was dramatic, and high as I was, I wouldn't let the dogs rip me apart. I stumbled out of the farmer's barn, where I had sought refuge from the maniacal attackers, crossed a fence, and fell into a muddy cornfield. I don't really recall going into the

barn, but I do remember the vicious dogs barking and snarling. I lost my shoes as I made my way across the cornfield.

I found myself in a mobile home park. I pounded on a door and someone answered. He must have witnessed or discerned my distress, because he invited me in to sleep it off. He apparently left his trailer, at which time I ransacked that poor man's belongings. When morning came, he pointed to my car across the field and even allowed me to telephone my girlfriend, oblivious to the violation of his trailer. What mercy!

The trips were getting worse and the scenarios becoming deadly. Again, I almost lost my life in the town of Riverton flirting with a woman. The jaws of Satan's insidious scheme were opening wide and I was the bait.

Most of my friends were making a wide path around me, and the remainder were being driven off because of my craziness.

The few that continued to associate with me were full fledged junkies or ex-felons.

Chapter Seven

THE REVELATION

"The wicked flee when no man pursueth; but the righteous are bold as a lion". Proverbs 28:1

The summer of 1975 was unforgettable.

Hallucinogens were easily obtained. I was tripping out every day and brushes with death had become commonplace, although I didn't grasp the gravity of these encounters. My sanity was slipping and episodes of blackouts and psychosis were frequent.

The weekend before the fateful day of Monday, August 4, 1975, I had scored a large quantity of PCP.

This is an animal tranquilizer, but also a street drug that is popular throughout America. It can be inexpensively manufactured and passed off under numerous names on the streets. Although it is used to tranquilize animals, it has just the opposite effect on humans. Some other dopers and I

shot this drug in our arms, snorted it, smoked it and diluted it in liquor. This particular weekend was one long psychotic episode. Where had my friends gone? My girlfriend took a trip to Texas to escape my insanity.

I went to the grocery store and made such a commotion that the police were summoned. I thought I was on camera and the whole incident was being videotaped. I began to ham it up and play my part not knowing that I was the only one in the script. They arrested me and I was taken to the drunk tank. I turned a paper cup upside down on the floor and set it ablaze. It left a round circular wax impression on the floor and blackened smoke. I drew a pentagram in the wax and stared at it. Although I was not deeply involved in witchcraft, I was not unfamiliar with the pentagram and what it represented. Many bands that I idolized embraced strong occult practices.

Later the same day I was released and went home. The PCP had worn off and a semblance of rationale had returned. The police thought I was coming down off a drunk and fined me twenty-five dollars for disturbing the peace. They also realized that a real basket case was in the drunk tank and didn't want to be responsible if I dove off the top bunk and killed myself. This episode at the supermarket and city jail was a definite catalyst that would expedite opening the door to demonic possession the following Monday morning.

The revelation came Monday morning.

Words cannot express the horror and fear that demonic spirits can generate in a man. Many times I had crossed over the threshold separating sanity from insanity. The bouts had always been induced through hallucinogens and alcohol. I always could return to some semblance of sanity as the effects of the drugs wore off. The devil controlled my spirit and body and was attacking the last vestige of resistance - my will! He was the puppeteer of darkness and I was his little man and he desired all of me; spirit, soul and body. I believe that a controlling spirit of murder entered into me that day just prior to my release from the drunk tank. Satan's plan was fulfilled as Frank Sherry was brought into total subjugation.

Confusion had plagued my apartment. Like little bees it seemed as if I was being stung with paranoia and fear. The rock music seemed to blend in with these eerie "noises" and sounds. The tangible things like plants and grass seemed to be made of plastic. Someone had reduced my apartment down to the bare minimum and even material was missing from my clothing. Nothing was real anymore. It was like I had been transported from the world as I knew it and placed in a "fake" and fictitious environment. It felt as if I was in a terrarium and unseen eyes were peering in and controlling my every move. Yes, indeed the conspiracy was unveiled and I had become aware of this trap. I was the rodent trapped in a maze of conspiracy. This human rodent would escape. I was on to the plot and subsequent invasion.

I heard voices speaking to me all weekend, but now they were intense and compelling. It was unmistakably a revelation concerning my imminent danger and ultimate survival. It was clear and concise. Alien entities had invaded Springfield and had captured the body, spirit, and soul of all life forms. Human, animal and plant life must be destroyed for they had been infested by this alien activity. These entities could read minds and knew that I "knew" of the plot and takeover. "You must escape and kill all living things in your path, for they are out to possess you; and since you are aware of this, they are also aware of your knowledge and are converging on you to possess your body".

Armed with a hammer, I began a murderous rampage destroying my cat and uprooting all the plants in the apartment.

I felt as if I was invincible. These aliens were feeble, and though they were mindful of my revelation, they would not be able to hinder my escape from Springfield. I attacked every person I saw with intent to kill and destroy. This was life or death and I was not going to give these alien beings an opportunity to capture me.

Insane or demon possessed individuals do not have reasoning abilities or constructive thought processes. In desperation, I got in my car to flee Springfield. I became aware of dehydration and stopped at a drug store for a drink. I immediately encountered the enemy - people!!! I continued the murderous assault. I demonstrated superhuman strength. The alien entities had no power over me but I became acutely aware that some of these entities were trying to resist me. Another revelation came! I would soon wear down and would be captured. Immediately, I broke a huge jar and with a thick piece of glass began gouging my left wrist and forearm. It was dull, but finally I gouged open my wrist exposing layers of flesh, arteries, and nerves. As the blood spurted from my self-inflicted gash, I recall the realization that my life was ending -- ebbing away, but I couldn't die fast enough. Capture was imminent and the aliens were upon me.

My last recollection in my semi-conscious state was severed arteries pumping my life out onto the drug store floor and dimmed voices. Blackness followed. I had escaped the tormentors!

Chapter Eight

COUNTY JAIL

"Our soul is escaped as a bird out of the snare of the fowler; the snare is broken and we are escaped." Psalm 124:7

Jails are not designed to be festive housing. I was highly experienced in spending the night or a weekend in jail, but never on a permanent basis. There is a jailhouse stench that I inevitably became accustomed to. Body odor permeates the atmosphere as well as human excrement. The floors are dirty and tacky. I never noticed it before in the short term, but some of the inmates actually were crazy. They were not playing with a full deck. Some clearly were homosexual, many were in for drug related activities, and others for murder or robbery. It was a menagerie. Even in my state of degradation I wasn't prepared for this. I was a small scale drug dealer housed with semi-professional and professional criminals. Homosexuals were blatant and active. It was disgusting, even to me. As the sun went down on the horizon, my future looked bleak. I was on the fifth floor and I couldn't go home.

Jails are literally small microcosms of society. Politics thrive and groups create their own little worlds and agendas. I remember one particular group with the "escape" agenda. It failed, but was something to talk about for a few days. Day after day created it's own particular enigma; boredom. I would have to be ingenious to overcome this monstrosity. My girlfriend visited from time to time, but our relationship was never the same. She would leave me a few dollars and that made me popular in the cell block.

One particular man use to cuss me out after the lights were out. He was a few cells away. I learned later that he was in and out of the Sangamon County Jail on many occasions. One day this man was thrown in the "hole". The hole has no sink or toilet facilities and no light. In fact, one is lucky to have a jumpsuit to wear and many have done a day or two without a stitch of clothing. There was, however, a small space under the steel door and cigarettes could be rolled through this space. My friend was in the hole and yelling for a square. A square is a cigarette and he was yelling at the top of his lungs. Being a humanitarian, I wanted to help him out but didn't know how to do it. He had just urinated in the small space under the door to show his defiance to the authority figures. The only thing that was in this black hole was a drain in the middle of the floor. I was somewhat perplexed. Was I to shoot a cigarette though this mess? Well, he cussed me out some more and said that there was no other way except to

come under the door. I obliged him.

As I mentioned before, the jails are filled with strange people and many of them have "bizarre" sexual tendencies. This man had the habit of flashing on me with his fits of lewdness and perversion. He also cussed me out after the lights were out. My last encounter with this man happened several months later and we were both in another section of the jail. He was up to his old homosexual tricks and I was getting mad. My adversary had pushed me to the limit and I stuffed his head down in the stainless steel toilet and begun to flush it several times. He was terrified and promised to walk lightly around me. He did too. Years later while I was in prison I heard that this man had gotten killed in Springfield. The irony of it was that his way of life never changed. The hole, days and weeks in the county jail; this was just a lifestyle that he had been accustomed to.

"The people who sat in darkness saw a great light; and them which sat in the region and shadow of death light is sprung up" Isaiah 9:2

It was in this county jail that reality began to filter through the fog of depression and despair seemingly at a snail's pace. The confusion was unbearable. Still deluded, the prospects of death seemed plausible. I could only hang my head in shame as the grand jury marched through my section of the jail promising revenge.

Sunday afternoons were usually action packed. Visitors came and football games on the television charged the atmosphere. A peculiar group of people came up on the cat walk just outside the bars every Sunday afternoon. They had smiles from ear to ear, and packed guitars and big bibles. I had never seen such big bibles. They were religious fanatics and talked about Jesus non-stop until their visit was over. They disturbed football games and I had enough on my mind without them compounding it with this fanaticism about Jesus. What could these "Jesus-Freaks" tell me? Why were they smiling and happy all the time? No one is that happy! When they came, I would stay in my small cell, but they still made too much noise. I could hear every word they uttered. I tried plugging my ears to avoid hearing their message.

What did they mean by becoming a "brand new creature" and being "born again?" Unnerved as I was, I found myself listening to their testimony and passages from the bible. These Christians came faithfully every Sunday afternoon and really believed in the "Good News" they preached.

My contempt changed to curiosity as I listened to the good news. Did God really love me? Why? I was a mass murderer, as I had learned one of the other men I attacked had also died. Could I be "born again?" Was there an authority and power higher than the drug addiction which had captured my soul for so many years? The remorse and distress plagued me. If I could only turn back the clock and start over again, I would do anything to reverse the course of action I had started at a young age.

The many years of drug addiction convinced me God was simply an illusion. He wasn't real and the masses that served Him were deceived. This planet had always been here. Yet, the words of these volunteer ministers were beginning to usher light into a darkened, aching soul. Hope was filtering in!

I rehearsed a unique phenomenon which had taken place weeks before. I remember lying in my bunk staring at the wall. I gazed at a crudely drawn cross etched on the back wall of my cell. In my transfixed state of mind, I heard a voice speak to me saying,

“SON THIS IS WHAT YOU ARE LOOKING FOR.”

I had heard this voice once before as a young child visiting with my family on my grandfather’s farm. The voice was so clear calling me “Son”, that I ran to my father to see if it was him calling.

Could this amazing tale of a God who shed His blood for Frank Sherry be true? It was incredibly difficult to believe.

Then an astounding incident occurred with an outcome that changed my life. I was informed that I had a visitor, although I wasn't expecting anyone. A small lady approached and a guard informed me that she was the

widow of one of the men I had killed and she wanted to see me. Mortification engulfed me. This lady introduced herself as Florence Dace and she held a huge black bible under her left arm. Remorse and self-condemnation flooded my soul as I faced her. Tears of contrition and shame filled my eyes as she began speaking to me. I couldn't look into her eyes because of the shame I felt.

"Frank", she said, "I am a Christian and my husband was a fine, upstanding man in the church and this community. He was an elder in the church and highly respected; now he is gone." She added, "Frank, the bible says that I must forgive you and the Lord has been telling me to come to the jail and speak with you." It was almost too much for both of us to bear, but she continued. "The bible says that, *'all things work together for good to them that love God, to them that are the called according to His purpose.' Romans 8:28.* I don't see how my husband's loss of life could ever work together for good, unless you become a minister, preach the gospel and bring life to those around you instead of death." We talked and shared for a brief time. I assured Florence that I would become a minister. I would have said anything to her in an effort to ease my conscience and her grief.

As Florence prepared to leave, she stretched forth her hand and handed me that huge bible, saying, "This was my husband's bible. Read it and it will change your life." She left and her visit became a catalyst that did change the destiny of my life.

Shortly after that visit and after a few more visits with the Christians, I experienced a mighty conviction to give my life to Jesus. I couldn't resist the tug of the Holy Spirit. On September 26, 1975, as I lay on my bunk, I said a simple prayer: *"Lord Jesus, if You are who they say You are, come into my life and make me a new creation. Forgive me for all my sins and set me free. I'm tired of this life I'm living and I want a new one. I will serve You all the days of my life"*

He came in and I was born again. The next morning, I knew I was saved. It wasn't long before a couple of the others in the cell block got saved. We began reading the bible and praying. I had never read the bible with such enthusiasm, which proved the change had come.

I bided my time with my fellow inmates, awaiting my hearing and trial as they did. After much prayer, I knew I was facing a lengthy sentence, but it was okay. All was well with my soul. After eight and one-half months in the Sangamon County Jail and a plea bargain of ten to thirty years, I was en route to a maximum security facility; Menard Correctional Center in Chester, Illinois. It was literally down the river.

Chapter Nine

THE JOINT

"...If you continue in my word, then are ye my disciples indeed; and, ye shall know the truth and the truth will make you free." **John 8:31-32**

The reception and classification (R & C) unit is the first place prisoners are sent. They are received and classified and assigned to one of the cell houses. The air is filled with nervous laughter and chatter. Stories of gang activity and rape dominate the conversation. Many prisoners choose the safety of protective custody (PC). Some have been in prison before and offer encouragement and advice. Newborn Christian or not, I considered fighting if necessary. Giving in to pressure and demands is the equivalent of being a punk or someone's lover.

As I walked into the East Cell House, the noise overwhelmed me. I heard at least fifty television sets and ghetto blasters blaring deafening and indistinguishable sounds at the same time. That cell house accommodated one thousand men.

As I gazed up at the tiers, I pondered my thirty year sentence. When I found my cell, I remember praying

silently, asking for His mercy and protection. Within 15 minutes after I entered the cell house I was approached by a gang member wanting to know the gang I was hooked up with. I was stunned at the quickness of this confrontation and managed to blurt out, "Jesus". My voice cracked and he laughed and walked away. He promised to come back. Of twenty men that went through classification, most of them were physically assaulted. At Menard Correctional Center, the "fresh fish" are open targets for the seasoned extortioners and "gang bangers". I was in a fight with two men within three days over a shower stall. It seemed as if this "fish" had picked the wrong shower. The biggest man was also on the boxing team, but I did fairly well.

My first two years at Menard were basically uneventful. I attended vocational school and worked toward an Associates Degree. It didn't occur to me that Jesus demanded the whole man. I went to church when I felt like it and read my bible occasionally. I had slipped back into some old drug associations. We made some stout prison "hooch" which was a treat for a Friday or Saturday night. Drugs were prevalent on the galleries and easily accessible.

Life droned on and my first two years quickly passed with my share of disciplinary tickets. When I appeared before the Adjustment Committee for a disciplinary infraction, I would always plead, "guilty with an explanation". The idea was to tell them the truth with hope of mercy. On many occasions, I had to pack my belongings

and move to segregation. When the cell was "shook down" and "hooch" or dope was found, one of us would plead guilty and take the weight; one going to the hole (segregation), and the other holding down the cell. My celly Rick and I, played that game for two and one-half years. One particular time I was put in the hole for a mishap over a guitar. The cell in segregation was the filthiest I had ever encountered. The stench was incredible.

The previous tenant had wallpapered the cell wall with toilet paper, urine and feces

In 1979, the Lord began to rustle my feathers. Groups were coming in from the streets talking about the power of God. I was beginning to hear about the infilling of the Holy Ghost. The Lord was dealing with me and beckoning me to come into the waters. He used one of my black friends as a mentor and guide. His name was James Barnes and we had attended some of the same vocational school classes. He was a genuine friend and companion. His secret weapon was his relationship with Jesus Christ. He motivated me to read the bible and search out the scriptures. After all, the bible did say, "*...if you continue in my word, then ye are my disciples indeed; and, ye shall know the truth and the truth shall make you free." (John 8:31,32)* I hadn't continued in the word since accepting Jesus Christ as my personal savior. This was a revelation. I was still bound by habits and sin.

The Spirit of the Lord began to deal with me concerning the mighty infilling of the Holy Ghost. I was reading a book that described this tremendous experience and it was bearing witness to my spirit. Also, the Spirit had me studying in the fourteenth through sixteenth chapters of St. John and other scripture pertinent to this infilling. I saw how the men in the book of Acts received this gift and it gave them the enabling power to preach and witness of the resurrection of Jesus Christ. I realized that I hadn't received this gift that was subsequent to salvation, and I wanted it. God is no respecter of persons and he is the same today as he was yesterday. Yes, I wanted to be filled with this precious and awesome gift.

One evening after the lights were out, I laid on my bunk and took a spiritual step of faith. I envisioned Peter stepping out of the boat to approach Jesus, and I took my step to approach the one who had died for me , saying:

"Lord Jesus, thank you for this marvelous gift. I receive it in the name of Jesus."

Instantly I was filled with the Holy Ghost and spoke with tongues as the Spirit gave utterance. Actually, I only spoke three syllables, but that was okay with me. Glory to God, I received the Holy Ghost and no demon in hell could convince me otherwise. The devil's accusations and harassment during the following weeks only deepened my conviction of this valid experience.

James and I became close friends and we lived and breathed the Word. James was a musician and the most talented, gifted virtuoso I ever had the pleasure of hanging around with. I, too, was a guitarist, so together we developed our musical skills. In spite of all the good things that God was doing, I had not recognized the significance of total commitment.

At the time I was in a southern rock group and we were beginning to get our sound together. One day as we were practicing, I noticed or perceived a particularly strong anointing on the last song we played. Everyone remarked that they had never heard me play so well. It was a strong demonic anointing! The same day the Lord spoke to my heart and said, "*Choose yea this day whom yea will serve*". The devil's insidious plan failed and I chose the Lord Jesus Christ. It was a good choice because one of my "jamming buddies" later got shot and killed after his release from prison.

Another associate was into satanic worship and hung himself in segregation.

James and I played music at the church from that day on. He eventually transferred out of Mend and the music director mantle fell on me. Something else was happening to me that had greater significance: *I realized that God had a calling on my life, thus fulfilling Sister Dace's prayer and heartfelt cry.*

Chapter Ten

THE DAY GOD STOPPED A RIOT

"Behold, I give you power to tread upon serpents and scorpions, and over all the power of the enemy: and nothing shall by any means hurt you." Luke 10:19

Riots in prison are deadly. It is commonplace to see one or more persons carted off to the infirmary or to the hospital. There were several riots during the six and one-half years I spent at Mend Correctional Center. Men were maimed, stabbed, and beaten.

Gangs often agitated one another over the simplest matter. Sometimes these small things escalated into full fledged riots. One such event happened that I will never forget.

The word was out (via the prison grapevine) that two of the large gangs were going to fight. This was to take place on the yard. I found myself going in that direction. I saw another Christian brother in the line and asked him why he was going out. He didn't know and I was equally dumbfounded as to why my legs were carrying me out to the yard. We were puzzled, yet had the strangest sensation, or leading, that we were supposed to be there.

We filed into the yard and I went to the right to walk around the track. My Christian brother went to the left. We were both praying fervently and with boldness. The air was thick with hostilities and we were in need of rapid guidance. Moment by moment the atmosphere was being charged with fear and hatred. I met my partner on the other side of the yard and asked him if the Lord had revealed anything to him. He said he felt led to go to the middle of the compound and pray. This was exactly what the Spirit prompted me to do.

We hastened to the middle of the yard and found ourselves between the two converging gangs. We were in the middle. We had walked right into a melee. I said, "Let's pray!" We fell to the ground and both began to pray. The last thing I saw before dropping to the ground was two seething gangs bent on destroying each other, and we were in between them.

We prayed like mighty prayer warriors and God heard our cries.

The gangs backed away from one another and the fight was averted. I'll never forget the day God stopped the riot.

God was moving in the prison and it was exciting. I recall getting the revelation that Jesus paid the full price for our redemption and that by His stripes we were healed. I walked down the gallery to see if anyone was in need of prayer. Men were getting saved, delivered and healed by the power of God. I laid hands on the cell house sergeant and prayed for his headaches.

One incident stands out in my mind that clearly demonstrated the power of God released. I recall praying for a man who was sick. His cell was open and I noticed nude pin ups and pornography all over the walls and cell. As I entered his cell, it was impossible not to see some form of nudity. When I prayed for the man, he opened his eyes and without prompting or suggestion, he began to rip the nude pictures and pornography off the walls. The Holy Ghost had brought conviction to this sinner and I had not said a word concerning this vice.

Spirit filled preaching and teaching helped us as young Christians get rooted and grounded in the Word of God. Several such ministries had great influence on my life. Jack Burbridge, *the Enforcer*, came to the prison three or four times a year and we were amazed at his boldness and witness for the Lord Jesus Christ. A.J. Magus, pastor of *Open Door Fellowship* in Alton, Illinois, held Wednesday morning bible classes which changed my life. Jesse Mattes and *Jesus is the Way Ministries* came in several times a year and encouraged us in a walk of faith and power. These men and ministries helped mold our walks and I can't say enough about the impact and influence they had on my life. These are just a few of the men and ministries that the Lord used mightily in prison ministry. To this day the above

mentioned men support us in our work of the Lord and we have ministered along side of them from time to time.

I had a Spirit filled warden at Menard Correctional Center. His name was Jim Greer. He ministered at one of the bible classes one morning. This is highly unusual but Warden Greed was a unique man of God. How many wardens do you know who are saved and filled with the Holy Ghost? He let us know that he could not handle his position as warden and chief administrator without the power of God activated in his life. I was so proud of him. He is now retired from the Department of Corrections and actively involved with prison ministry.

I worked in the chaplaincy department and the Spirit of the Lord alerted me that something was going down in the incoming mail. The chaplains were ready and a plot was uncovered which revealed a secret smuggling operation. One of the gangs was trying to bring in large quantities of marijuana in boxes of bibles. Picture that!

A program was initiated to bring the Christian inmates and Christian staff and officers together. This was revolutionary. This program helped significantly to bridge the gap between prison staff and inmates. Employees and residents were touched as the power of God moved during these fellowship meetings. Many walls crumbled as staff and prisoners grasped the significance of "... ***there is neither bond nor free, there is neither male nor female: for ye are all one in Christ Jesus.*****" (*****Galations 3:28*****)**

The bible says, "... ***we are changed into the same***

image from glory to glory..." (2 Corinthians 3:18) My counselor called me in his office in late 1982 and suggested that it might be an appropriate time to request a transfer. When inmates keep their nose clean and maintain a good record, they are transferred to better institutions with more privileges and liberties.

Granted, I had my share of disciplinary tickets during my first two years, but I was free from disciplinary infractions after putting the Lord in charge of my life. I hastily told my counselor, "Yes! Put me in!" I later repented because I had not sought the Lord's counsel concerning this. I then made it right with the Lord. "Lord, if it is your will for me to transfer, then open the door, and if not, close it." I did want this transfer and prayed that it would come through for me. From that moment on, it was in the Lord's hands. I pondered one day whether or not I would be granted this transfer, and I heard my mouth speak these words, "I'll believe it when I see it."

The Spirit immediately spoke to me that we are a people that"...walk by faith and not by sight."

When the bus pulled in to transfer me to Hillsboro, Illinois, I was elated. It hadn't been too long since I had wept tears as my best friend, James Barnes, had transferred and now, it was my turn.

God was performing a great and mighty work in my life and I was thankful. I knew without a doubt that there was a calling upon my life. Warden Greer had given me free reign at Menard to minister the Word. Many men had come to the Lord, but my season at Menard was now complete. I don't regret a single day.

As I boarded the transfer bus, my mind and spirit flooded with seemingly thousands of thoughts and memories of the power of God in action in a tough maximum security prison. He had done so much and yet I knew that it was only the beginning. Good-bye Menard! Many times I had prophesies that my next trip to Menard would be different. The next time I would be ministering and preaching the gospel as a respected minister.

After my departure the mantle fell on a young man named James Treptow and only time would tell of the tremendous effect that this brother would have upon Menard Correctional Center. It was powerful.

Jim was my celly and not particularly on fire for Jesus when I first met him. I had helped him get a job in the chaplaincy department. Little did I know that this gesture of friendship would eventually help with an inside ministry that would span 20 years.

I recall once as we prayed kneeling on the cell floor, he fell asleep. I laughed silently not realizing that this man would impact two prisons in a mighty way. He has led many to the Lord and affected both inmate and administration. He will be released in September 2000, after serving out his full 20 year sentence.

Chapter Eleven

GRAHAM CORRECTIONAL CENTER

"For promotion cometh not from the east, nor from the west, nor from the south. But God is the judge; he putteth down one, and setteth up another." **Psalm75:6-7**

What happened to the walls? Graham Correctional Center didn't have monster cell houses or walls. It was only about seven years old and appeared like a college campus. It was a medium security facility and they didn't march in lines either. I liked it at first glance. Some of my closest Christian brothers had transferred there and I felt like the rapture had taken place. The atmosphere was relaxed and the facilities were geared for the campus look.

I found my friend, James Barnes, and another brother I hadn't seen in five years named Jimmy Williams. It was at this facility that the Lord began to speak to us to begin a new phase in our Christian walk, to establish the five-fold ministry. This ministry would include elders and deacons. If there was a pastor, teacher, or prophet that was proven and above reproach, then he would be ordained and acknowledged. The Lord assured us that it was critical at

this time so the younger Christians could acknowledge them and submit to them in matters of wisdom, prayer, etc. This was the Lord's work as we could more adequately minister to those who recognized the gifts and callings in the ministry.

The guards tried breaking up our yard meetings because they were ignorant of our intentions. Sometimes they were just plain ornery. Gang members often congregated in groups and would be broken up. The gangs were either all black, all white, or Hispanic. Our Christian meetings included all colors. God is no respecter of persons and saves all races, peoples, and creeds. Our fellowship was a conglomeration of colors and races. We had some fine meetings and the Body of Christ began to come together in unity.

Brother Barnes left first for the minimum security prison at Vienna. I was the next to leave, and finally Brother Jimmy William's. Once more the Lord was taking us into another realm and I was excited. *"For promotion cometh not from the east, nor the west, nor from the south. But God is the judge; he putteth one down and setteth up another." (Psalms 75: 6-7)*

It was May 1985, and I had been incarcerated for nearly ten years. This was the last step before freedom. I had seen the parole board five times and had been denied five times. I had learned that although I am not always happy, I am full of the joy of the Lord, and that joy is the strength of my life.

Chapter Twelve

VIENNA CORRECTIONAL CENTER

"In all thy ways acknowledge him and he shall direct thy paths." *Proverbs 3:6*

Vienna was called the country club of the Illinois Department of Corrections. This facility was enormous and encompassed hundreds of acres in southern Illinois. There was a huge lake where we were allowed to fish on the weekends. The fresh fish sure beat the rectangular fish we had eaten for years, not to mention the "shrimp shapes", whatever they were.

Vienna actually had a golf course. There were no greens or holes, but the field was big, and Leisure Times Activities (LTA) supplied woods and irons. We had two annual Holy Ghost Invitationals. My golfing ended one day when I hooked an iron shot into the weight lifting area. That was a blunder because weight lifters in prison were a close resemblance to world professional wrestlers, and acted like them too. I retired from golfing that day.

The only requirement at Vienna Correctional Center was to come in for head count. I thanked and praised the

Lord for such abundant blessings. The freedom and liberty to fish or golf opened many doors to witnessing and sharing the love of Jesus throughout the prison. God was so good to me.

Throughout this entire prison experience, God had always provided opportunities for me to get the best jobs available. At Menard, I had been a plumber after my schooling and graduation from college and vocational school. In the medium security facility at Graham, I completed the electrical maintenance course and was made the electrician's assistant, a job I didn't even ask for. When I went to the Assignment Committee, I thought I was going to the furniture shop. God had other plans, and I was assigned a 24 hour on call electrician's assistant position. This made the whole prison accessible for witnessing for Jesus.

Vienna was no exception. God opened the door and I got the best paying job in the facility. Once again, God had promoted me and I was making more money than anyone, working on the farm. The only exception to this was the other 5 farmers that worked out on the farm. Glory! I could clearly see that the hand of the Lord was upon my life and he was the one that caused the favor to come.

During the month of August 1985, a singing group called New Life came into the prison. This was a fantastic Spirit-filled ministry and Ruth Roberts was among the singers. I had previously met Sister Ruth at Menard Correction Center, as she was involved in prison ministry.

The fact was, she had actually opened and answered some of my letters written to an evangelist she worked with. My path crossed Sister Ruth's mostly through correspondence and I knew her as a sister in the Lord. Years before the Lord had spoken to me that she was a virtuous woman. I assumed that the Lord was pointing out what type of woman he wanted me to someday marry; one full of faith and virtue, such as Ruth.

I knew Ruth would be in this particular meeting and wanted to see my friend and sister in the Lord. We knew many of the same prison ministers and friends, so this was par for the course and I was excited. Throughout the years I had cultivated some dear friendships with sisters in the Lord. When I thought that the relationship was getting serious, I would always stop it. This happened on several occasions.

I recall asking Ruth somewhat awkwardly if she ever planned on getting married some day. I tried sounding comical and rhetorical, but was taken aback by her answer: "Yes, in God's time." I mused over this reply. Little did I know, this was the dawn of a fiery romance.

The service was great and I escorted Sister Ruth to the bus and some of the other Christian inmates helped get the equipment loaded. The feelings I felt were peculiar.

Sister Ruth and I corresponded frequently and the situation heightened. What was wrong with me? I rebuked the devil time and time again thinking that someone had put a "love spell" on me. I began to dream about this woman. I

dreamed that she was knocking at my door. (Vienna Correctional Center had individual rooms with doors) What was going on? I understood lust from my years as a heathen, but this was different. Was this my bride to be?

We had a music ministry at Vienna and were blessed to have the privilege to minister outside the prison at churches, picnics, and special events. This ministry was unique in that few prisons in America have programs allowing prisoners to go out and minister to the free world. Ruth, on occasion, would meet us at these churches and this set the stage for a visit to Warden Jim Greer's office.

Warden Greer was a very unique man. I had known him from the very beginning at the maximum security facility in Menard. He was a Christian and full of the Holy Ghost. His job was very hard and the daily pressures were enormous; yet he maintained a faithful witness, and I respected him highly. Now he was warden at Vienna.

The warden asked, "Frank, are you getting sweet on Ruth?" I stood in front of his desk and gulped.

It is during these critical times that our faith stands the tests.

Many thoughts raced through my mind as I pondered this question. He continued, "They frown on prison relationships with volunteers." Did I detect a glimmer in his eyes? My reply was that I was very much in love with Ruth, and I was told I'd have to make a decision;

either she would quit as a volunteer and be placed on my visiting list, or she couldn't visit.

Ruth and I began a budding courtship in the visitor's room every Saturday and Sunday. I thrived on those visits.

I was in love and God had given me a virtuous woman as my companion in ministry.

We were even blessed to attend services together at the chapel in Vienna. This was another benefit at this particular correction facility.

We read the bible through two and one-half times and ministered to folks in the visitor's room. We practiced some songs and got on the guards' nerves. They did not comprehend how prisoners could be so happy and full of joy.

Vienna Correctional Center was the last stop in my twelve and one-half year prison term. I never made parole but maxed or flat-timed my 30 year sentence. I considered it a miracle to get out so quickly. The sixteenth chapter of Mark's gospel became a living reality to me. Most of my closest and dearest friends had callings on their lives. Some were out of prison and preaching the gospel. I preached, taught, and evangelized at Vienna Correctional Center until the day of my release.

Chapter Thirteen

OUT OF PRISON

"And he changed his prison garments; and he did eat bread continually before him all the days of his life. And his allowance was a continual allowance given him of the king, a daily rate for every day, all the days of his life."

II Kings 25:28-29

The snow was falling the morning of February 11, 1988. I was like a man dreaming. "*...the Lord looseth the prisoner." (Psalms 146:7)* After twelve and one-half years in prison, it seemed like a dream. Was it true?

Ruth and I were married seven months earlier in the prison chapel, and now she was here to take me home. As we drove out of Vienna Correctional Center, all the Christian brothers were waving at us. It was awesome!

A huge ranch style house was awaiting us rent free. A ministry that we were affiliated with provided the house and it was ours to use. God takes care of His own. The house was so big that it took me some time to simply adjust to the spaciousness.

Getting use to higher prices, balancing checkbooks,

driving cars, and financial management seemed somewhat difficult at first. However; the transition went rather well.

Every prisoner battles this fear of uncertainty or failure shortly before release.

My wife helped me tremendously and supported me with encouragement. The combination of a strong relationship with my wife and with Jesus proved to be the catalyst for a smooth transition in the free world. A strong relationship with Jesus is the foremost factor for success in anyone's life.

My associations in prison made me "Body" minded. *"For as the body is one, and hath many members, and all the members of that one body, being many, are one body: so also is Christ." (1 Cor. 12:12) "And God hath set some in the church, first apostles, secondarily prophets, thirdly teachers, after that miracles, then gifts of healings, helps, governments, diversities of tongues." (1 Cor. 12:28)*

Ruth had recently moved to the area and occupied this ministry house. We would worship together in the prison chapel on Sundays. The bible says that God is building his church, and we immediately sought a place where God wanted us to worship. The Lord began to move in our lives and many churches opened their doors to allow me to minister and share my testimony.

One such church was *Open Door Fellowship* in Alton, Illinois. The pastor of the church, A. J. Maggos, was a

minister that I esteemed highly in the Lord. Brother Maggos had faithfully taught bible class every Wednesday at Menard Correctional Center. I had encountered the power of God in his bible classes and respected this man. He was a father and spiritual overseer in my life. Before we realized it, we were packing our belongings and moving to Alton to be a part of this glorious fellowship.

Through *Open Door Fellowship*, God opened the door for me to attend ministry classes and make preparations for full-time ministry. I knew there was a call on my life to minister, but I had not realized the full scope of that calling. I knew while I was in prison the Lord had given me the heart of a pastor.

My wife and I were happy with our new home. God had provided good jobs for us, and we began to learn valuable lessons in working together as a husband and wife team. We learned to always have peace about our decisions and to be in agreement.

Quality decisions that are in His will are always followed by peace.

The Lord continued to open opportunities for us to minister and share my testimony in other churches and fellowships.

Chapter Fourteen

RETURN TO PRISON

"When the Lord turned again the captivity of Zion, we were like them that dream." *Psalms 126:1*

My heart's desire was to return to the maximum security prison at Menard Correctional Center and minister to the men there.

I knew it would have to be a supernatural act of God because I was still on parole and it was an impossible situation within the prison system.

My wife and I learned that a friend of ours, Jack Burbridge; also an ex-convict, was scheduled to minister at a small church in Chester, Illinois. This church was close to Menard and we had a notion that Warden Greer might be at this service. The warden and Jack were close friends also. We felt that the Spirit of the Lord would have us to attend this special service.

As we arrived at the church and were meeting new friends and talking with Jack and his wife, the church door opened and in walked Warden Jim Greer. We began to hug

each other and weep. What a beautiful sight!

Only God performs a miracle uniting a convict and a warden, knitting their spirits as one.

Warden Greer signed a special authorization allowing my wife and I to return to Menard, not only on a one time basis, but to minister weekly in bible study and on many occasions in the chapel.

This time when the prison gates automatically locked behind me, it was an overwhelming emotional experience. The guards were calling me Mr. Sherry and I knew that indeed, our God is a mighty God.

As I entered the meeting room that first night, it was packed. The men had heard that I was coming back. The Spirit of God moved in a powerful demonstration of love and forgiveness. Many were saved that night and filled with the Spirit as my wife and I proclaimed,

"...the Lord looseth the prisoner." (Psalms 146:7)

We went through the prison orientation program and drug testing to be recognized as volunteer prison chaplains. To date, we are still active in prison ministry and have held services in other prisons across the states. We have maintained our relationship with Warden Jim Greer over the years and he has become an extraordinary brother in the Lord.

Chapter Fifteen

RETURN TO SPRINGFIELD

"And we know that all things work together for good to them that love God, to them who are the called according to his purpose."

Romans 8:28

One day I received a letter from the pastor of a large church in Springfield, Illinois, requesting me to come and share my testimony with that congregation. It was not unusual to receive such a request as news of my release, and the wonderful works the Lord had done in my life, had spread.

What was unusual about this request was that it came from Sister Daces' pastor. Sister Florence Dace -- big bible -- Sangamon County Jail, 1975! We had talked about the significance of such a meeting years before but now it was becoming reality. It was no easy decision to make, so I called on the Lord who gave me strength and a supernatural anointing. How would I be received in this congregation? I was, in the eyes of many, an unregenerate man -- a murderer deserving of death.

Words cannot describe the emotions I experienced on the drive to Springfield, Illinois.

The pastor did not announce my coming prior to the time. As he called my name and I was introduced, my knees began to shake and nearly buckled. My tongue seemed to cleave to the roof of my mouth. As I turned to face the congregation, I saw hundreds of people looking at me. Sister Dace came and stood by my side as I ministered. The Spirit of God moved through that congregation and healed many struggling with their own accounts of unforgiveness. I shared my testimony of deliverance in two services that day, and; to the glory of God, was well received. A newspaper reporter was in one of the meetings and the following day an entire column appeared giving the account of my return to Springfield. The column was accurate and well written. Ironically, the only objections concerning this momentous day, came from the Illinois Department of Corrections. The Prisoner Review Board was nervous because they couldn't comprehend this turn of events.

We continue our relationship with Sister Dace and her pastor. As with Joseph in the Old Testament, what Satan tried to use to destroy my life, God was able to turn it around to the good. The bible tells us in Romans 8:28, "*For all things work together for good to them that love God, to them who are the called according to his purpose*", just as Sister Dace had explained to me so many years before.

Chapter Sixteen

PASTOR SHERRY

"Brethren, I count not myself to have apprehended: but this one thing I do, forgetting those things which are behind, and reaching forth unto those things which are before, I press toward the mark for the prize of the high calling of God in Christ Jesus." *Philippians 3:13*

Carl Seago, a close friend who had been incarcerated with me had moved to Arkansas. He and his wife sent us a letter inviting us to come and share our testimony in their church. We were enthusiastic to see our friends and to meet new friends. Sherry, his wife, had ministered to the men at Vienna Correctional Center with a singing group called *Sonshine.*

There is an old saying concerning Arkansas: "If you visit more than two times, the third time you bring your furniture." We fell in love with the beautiful hills, surrounding lakes and tranquil countryside. Most of all, we fell in love with the people.

The little church that we ministered in was praying for a pastor. It was a strong fellowship that had developed

through a bible study.

We were invited back several times over a period of three years, and with each visit it became harder to leave. The decision to move to Heber Springs and accept the pastorate was not an easy one. Emotions ran high. We were torn with mixed feelings. Our allegiance to Pastor A. J. Maggos and the Body at *Open Door Fellowship* was inextricable, but the Spirit was ever tugging and pointing us toward Arkansas. God had miraculously brought us to *Open Door Fellowship*, but now he was redirecting us south. After lengthy consultation, we departed Alton, Illinois with Brother Maggo's tears, blessings and prayers. Praise God!

Our God is indeed an awesome God. If you will be faithful to hold fast, he will be faithful to bring it to pass. God can and will set the captive free. He never fails. He is King of kings and Lord of lords. He is more powerful than drug addiction, alcoholism, homosexuality, or any other power in heaven or on earth. God loved this murderer who was filled with unclean devils. I was possessed by these entities, but Jesus set me free and delivered me. He can do it for you also. His power is greater than fear, depression, guilt, or rejection. He loves you. He is omnipotent. His power is greater than gang activity and workers of iniquity.

The Lord Jesus Christ took a bewildered and confused drug addict and murderer, and made him a highly respected minister. He restored to me the years that the enemy destroyed.

If you mean business with Jesus, He will mean

business with you. You can fulfill the "great commission". You'll speak with new tongues, cast out devils and lay hands on the sick and see them recover. You will then walk in victory. Sin will no longer have dominion over you. You will know the truth and the truth will make you free. The joy of the Lord will be your strength. He is the Way, the Truth and the Life. He will set you on high and cause you to abound. Victory is yours. Receive Jesus as Savior and Lord and you will understand what it means to be "Born Again".

EPILOGUE

"...Go home to thy friends, and tell them how great things the Lord has done for thee, and hath had compassion on thee."
Mark 5:19

God is an awesome God and He has a plan for each and every one of us. When we give our life to Him, He has promised to direct our paths. It is marvelous to behold the plan of God unfolding before us.

The move to Arkansas opened many doors for us to minister in the prisons. Jack Burbridge, from *Crime to Christ Ministries,* who so faithfully had visited and ministered to me was now our neighbor. He told us he had a surprise and invited us to lunch. We found that Dennis Pigman, who had been one of my chaplains at Menard Correctional Center in Illinois, was now the head chaplain at Tucker Correctional Center in Arkansas. "Please come and share your testimony to the men on Death Row," Chaplain Pigman said. "I know they will respond to your story." I was happy to do this, and began visiting Tucker Prison on a regular basis.

It was also Jack Burbridge who introduced us to Dennis Wilson of *Word of Victory Prison Ministries* in Helena, Arkansas. Dennis was instrumental in opening the doors for us to minister in the 6,000 man prison complex in

Parchman, Mississippi. The first meeting we had at Parchman with Dennis was in Unit 26. It was the catalyst that caused us to answer the call to full time prison ministry. We saw a deaf ear opened, a crooked back straightened and many men filled with the Holy Ghost. Dennis Wilson is now the senior chaplain at the Tucker Unit in Arkansas. We have been working together ever since.

The move to Arkansas opened many doors for us to minister in the prisons. Although we loved the church and pastorate, our hearts began to stir for those locked up behind bars. Isaiah 14 tells us how the devil has made the world a wilderness and he refuses to loose his prisoners.

Only Jesus can set us free.

Requests began coming to us, asking me to come and share my testimony in the prisons. Doors began to open in Michigan, Mississippi, Tennessee, Oklahoma, Alabama and Illinois.

Time and time again it was confirmed to us that God was calling us into full-time prison ministry. God clearly spoke to my heart:

"...Go home to thy friends, and tell them how great things the Lord has done for thee, and hath had compassion on thee." Mark 5:19

The transition of pastor to prison evangelist was not

an easy decision, but the Spirit was controlling the situation. On May 26, 1992, we incorporated *The Lord Looseth the Prison Ministries.* Since that time, we have shared this testimony to thousands in schools, churches, prisons and other fellowships. Ruth and I have been guests on many radio and television programs including *The 700 Club, 100 Huntley Street, Messianic Vision, and Cornerstone Television.* God has moved tremendously and confirmed His word with signs and wonders following.

Statistics can be misleading but we really rejoice when we see the results of this ministry. One such man that was saved in Mississippi was a high ranking gang member in one of the largest gangs in this nation. He gave his heart to the Lord and resigned his rank and membership. He now declares that Jesus is his Lord and Savior.

We minister to thousands and rejoice when we witness the transforming power of God to save, deliver and heal. Deaf ears have been opened and miracles have been wrought. God is moving in the prisons across this nation.

I often weep as I see the men file in for a service. I can relate to their feelings and situations. I see their faces and feel the anguish of their soul when I lay down at night. I've been there! It is this connection that creates a rapport and mutual trust between the men and the ex-con. They relate to me because I have walked in their shoes. And God has anointed me for this specific job.

The percentage that lay hold of eternal life is not overwhelming, but the Spirit is there in a profound and

significant way.

Sister Dace has left a legacy behind as she boldly declared, *"You have to forgive"*. Jesus tells us in Luke 6:37, *"forgive and ye shall be forgiven."* Unforgiveness can destroy us. She went home to be with the Lord in August 1997. Her simple act of obedience has resulted in thousands being impacted by this ministry.

April 3, 1993, we were scheduled to speak at a Full Gospel Businessmen's dinner in Springfield, Illinois. Prior to the meeting a man approached me and wanted to introduce himself.

He was the officer who had arrested me on the fateful night of August 4, 1975.

Now a born again Christian, God allowed us to minister together. He explained how the night of the arrest, he had seen me dying in my own pool of blood and for an instant he and the other officers considered letting me die. But God had mercy and allowed me to live and show forth his lovingkindness. At another meeting with this same group in 1999, we met a nurse who had assisted at the hospital when I was brought in after the suicide attempt in the drug store. She told us that when she saw me that she whispered a prayer for me.

Each day we see new mercies of God extended to us. I am thankful for all those from the past that have seen the awesome change that God has wrought in my life. I am thankful for all the individuals, families, pastors and ministries that have played such a valuable role in my life. I am indebted to all.

Often I am asked , especially by young people, "what about the other victims?" I would like to say that with the exception of the other man who died, I do not know who the other victims were. That information was not given to me other than their names. I have not pursued any follow up, choosing to believe that God can create the right opportunities and the right time. I believe God in His infinite wisdom will allow me the opportunity to express myself to the other victims in His own time. I paid my debt to society and it is my heartfelt prayer that those affected by this crime will find forgiveness in their heart for me.

We believe that the coming of the Lord is drawing nigh. If you have not accepted Him as your Lord and Savior, don't wait another minute. The bible tells us that "*...today is the day of salvation.*"

Just pray this simple prayer with a repentant heart. "Lord Jesus, I know that I am a sinner and I need to be saved. Come into my life and cleanse me of my sin. I believe that you are the Son of God and the Savior of the world. I believe that you died on the cross for the salvation of all mankind. I receive You into my heart. In Jesus name. Amen."

A Simple Act

Thirty years or life, the choice was his to make.
He could sign and do the time, or a jury choose his fate.
He made some stupid choices when he chose the life of crime,
Now the drugs weren't talking, "Show me where to sign".
The depth of God's forgiveness was shown to him one day.
The widow of his victim came by the jail to say:
"Take my husband's bible, and read where in the word, all things work for good, to those that love the Lord."

The end from the beginning, tomorrow from today,
God knows who'll take His offer, who'll turn Him away.
Christ will take the vilest soul and wash away the sin.
Choose either hell or Jesus, you must be born again.

Who could know a life would change from such a simple act:
A bible from a widow, a scripture proven fact?
He shared his testimony and finally understood,
What Satan meant for evil, God can turn to good.
It doesn't matter where you are or what bad things you've done.
The truth is: God so loved the world that He sent His only Son,
Who gave His life to save you when you call upon His name.
He makes everyone the offer and loves everyone the same.

The end from the beginning, tomorrow from today,
God knows who'll take His offer, who'll turn Him away.
Christ will take the vilest soul and wash away the sin.
Choose either hell or Jesus, YOU MUST BE BORN AGAIN!

Bill Pierce
Great Hope Evangelism
Louisville, Kentucky

INMATE TESTIMONIES

William Holly

My name is William Holly. I am an inmate on Death Row in the state of Mississippi. But more importantly, I am a follower of the Lord and Savior, Jesus Christ.

My introduction to the reality and ability of Jesus began while I was being held in a city jail awaiting trial on multiple felony charges. But my introduction to Jesus unfortunately did not produce within me a lasting commitment to Him or His ways. Not being grounded on His Word and not having an understanding of what being a follower of Jesus really meant, just as quickly as I came to know Him, I turned from Him and back to the world and all its ways.

It was not until my coming here to Death Row that my introduction to the reality of Jesus, and now also His very persistent witnesses like Frank Sherry and Dennis Wilson, began to actually affect my life, and also the lives of those around me.

I began to dig into the bible, and was given fellowship and guidance by such people once again as Frank Sherry and Dennis Wilson, and began to get "rooted" with Jesus and my commitment to Him (slowly, very slowly but surely.) Whereas now, I'm going and growing with Him!

It wasn't until several months later that I received the Baptism of the Holy Spirit; yet again through Frank

Sherry. (He seems to pop up a lot in this doesn't he?)

And to date, it has been now five years consistently pursuing (not without stumbling along the way) the walk of faith, following Jesus. I've had my share of both troubles, persecutions, testings, denied appeals, near executions among other things, but also my share of triumphs, victories and answered prayers. I am not a compulsive liar anymore. I do not steal anymore. I have seen my family come into a relationship with Jesus, and experienced the blessing of leading others to Christ. All in all, I wouldn't trade it for nothing.

Louis Scott

My name is Louis Scott #31646, AKA Big Ku, and AKA Satan. I was born in New Orleans, Louisiana, September 1, 1951. I was raised in the Magnolia Projects in New Orleans. I have been involved in gangs most of my life. I am doing life plus 30 years in the Mississippi Department of Corrections in Parchman, Mississippi. I have already served 21 years of my sentence; much of it has been in solitary confinement. (Before coming to Parchman, I served 3 years and 8 months in the federal prison system.) I have been the highest-ranking officer in the Black Gangster Disciples since being at Parchman. I've had over a thousand soldiers at my beck and call. I was ruthless and proud of it. I slang (pushed) dope more than many surrounding small towns and cities. I ran prostitution rings with homosexuals and free world women. Protection, extortion, free world booze and anything you can think of to hitting for hire. We were into it and I called the shots.

In 1990, (I don't remember the month) a group of Christians came to the unit I was in and were going around talking to convicts and praying. I usually had Christians on my "pay me no mind" list because all you see in prison is people who use Christianity as a way to get out early or get an easy job. But this man, Frank Sherry walked up to me and looked me in the eyes (a feat in itself because most people cringe from eye contact with me) and said, "Brother, do you know Jesus loves you?" He shook my hand; I was dumb struck. I usually have some smart retort at this point but I just stood there like a fool trapped by this man's eyes that showed no fear whatsoever, only love. He led me around talking to me and asking questions, which in itself caused quite a stir among the inmates. This has never been done before. It was like a preacher and the devil walking around and holding a civil conversation!

One Christmas they were handing out snacks in the kitchen and I just went to look. At that time, I never took anything from the Christians when they came around. My reasoning was I didn't believe what they taught and I wasn't going to be one of those who sang praises to the Lord as long as you were passing out cakes and pops; then when you left, go back to the dope bag or buck or their punk or their man. I made up my mind to be the same each day of my life, even when I was wrong, I would never fake. I'd always keep it real.

About this time, I started having health problems. I was 6 ft. tall, 380 pounds and an accomplished martial artist and had a work out program that lasted 6 hours a day with as many as 30 or 40 convicts participating. My problem was diabetes, which I completely ignored. I refused being put on insulin and the doctors told me I was going to die. I had my pick of everything, the Queens (homosexuals that dress up like women) dope, cash, etc. But I was sick and feeling bad and the youngsters coming off the streets were a different breed. Crack babies; no respect, no principles, and no sense. Most of them turned out to be punks because they didn't know how to be men.

I started getting sicker, throwing up every day, high blood pressure, high sugar. I started reading the bible. Then I got a chance to see Brother Frank and Sister Ruth Sherry again. They were bringing in Christmas treats. I really was glad to see them. I helped them pack up and set up the food and stuff. I really wanted to get Brother Frank off by himself and tell him how I was feeling in my heart and ask him if he thought Jesus could love someone like me; but I was so ashamed. I still wanted to know about Jesus so I started attending services at the Spiritual Life Center (the church at Parchman built by inmates) every week and listening to the sermons. I got sick in July of 1996 and had to be hospitalized; my bladder burst. I began to pray. I got down on my knees (for the first time in my life) and prayed to Jesus for help. I had demons inside of me. I had learned many forms of devil worship over the years and my body is covered with brands (tattoos) that pay homage to Satan and his rule on earth. I prayed to Jesus to bring me out of the hands of Satan and to change my ways. Brother Frank showed up and prayed for me. It was really strange that the same day I went to the hospital, he showed up. He laid hands on me and I can say that was the day I was saved, that I truly accepted Jesus Christ as my Lord and Savior, no ifs, and or buts.

I gave my life to Jesus Christ in September of 1996. I am witnessing and working with young people here at Parchman to show them that following God's rules don't make them weak or square. It takes a real warrior to live a happy, healthy and productive life in Jesus name. God bless you. I am free on the inside.

TEXAS YOUTH RECEIVES LIFE

Jesse Robert Furr/Stanley

My life as a child was one of the best a kid could ever want. My mom was the best mom in the world, but my step-dad was real hard on me and my older brother. I always thought my step-dad hated us, but in reality he was trying to treat us like men and worked us like men. Trying to teach us to support ourselves. But as a kid of only 10 years I thought he did it out of hatred. So, as I grew up I began to hate because I didn't realize what my step-dad was trying to do. I would run away from home, stay out late or just not come home at all on school nights. It was all about going

out with my friends, doing drugs, getting drunk and fighting anything that would look at me wrong. People around San Angelo, Texas and Grape Creek, Texas, just outside of San Angelo called my friends and I "The Grape Creek Wild Bunch". It seemed like my mom would have to come get me out of jail every night for fighting or public drunkenness. Every time I went to jail it would make my step-dad mad. I thought I was paying my step-dad back for all the hatred I thought he was giving me. It was much later in life that I realized what he was trying to teach me...I finally moved to Arkansas to get away from everyone, but nothing changed except, I couldn't get drugs because I was a new guy in town and no one would sell to me because no one knew me. This only led to more drinking since booze was the only thing I could get. One day while I was drinking with a good buzz going, a family member and myself were talking about money problems we were having. This person was my step-mom. My dad and her wanted me to stay to help them out with paying rent, but I wanted to get my own place. I told my step-mom, "if you all are having that much trouble with money, why not sell these guns to help out"? I started playing with one of the guns, pointing it around in the room. I shouldn't have been doing that and the gun went off and killed my step-mom. I was arrested and put in jail. Three months later I was sentenced to life in prison. After I was sentenced to life, I grew up real fast. I had too. I was now living in a bad man's world (prison). I wanted to hurt someone because I thought my step-dad put me in this place

and the only people around I could hurt were fellow inmates. This revenge and rage was taken out on the inmates that I came into contact with. I can remember a time when five inmates jumped me. They thought they had the advantage on me because of sheer numbers. It was five to one.

What they didn't know was that I had a 4 foot 2x2 oak stick and one of my friends close by. Well we had our little fight and several of them got hurt. My associate got shanked with a homemade knife. After this, my friends and I formed a Brotherhood group. After a few years of hurting folks and the fact that I did my job so good, I gained the position of Captain of Arms. Every time we had to go out, you can bet someone was going to get hurt. One day we were going to make a hit on three inmates. Two of them had stolen from a member of our organization and the other was foolish enough to put a contract out on one of our members.

My friend, who was the target, and I went after the guy who paid the contract. This turned out to be a bloody day and caused me to be shipped to Tucker Maximum Security. I guess my actions could be likened to the Apostle Paul who thought he was doing right before Jesus revealed himself to him. Paul defended his beliefs with a passion and I was like that in our organization. I had to be champion and tone setter for our organization and we had it going.

So here I am at Tucker Max, in Arkansas, locked down in a single man cell. I guess one could say I've had

plenty of time to think about what I did. One day my mom and step-dad came to see me and something in me felt strange. It wasn't because of them because they had come many times before, but I still couldn't figure out what was bothering me. When I went out there it didn't strike me right off but later I was looking at my mom and she looked sad and my step-dad didn't look much better. I asked them what was going on and why were they looking so down. My dad said, "Son, we have been thinking of you and we want you to know that we love as well as miss you very much". Well, I didn't know if I should cry or laugh at him, but what happened caught me off guard. I told him that I loved him too.

Later that night I got to thinking of what went on and what I said to my dad and what he said to me and the feelings I had during the visit. It was puzzling to me because these emotions were new to me. I had learned to hate and bitterness ruled my soul. One day while out watching TV, I noticed two men in the barracks. A friend of mine told me they were volunteer chaplains who come to the unit and pray with inmates. I thought to myself, "Man, I've got to get away from these guys!" While I was thinking this they were on their way over to talk to me. When they sat down they introduced themselves as Frank Sherry and Robert McGhehey. What they said was going in one ear and out of the other. Right before they got up to leave I said something that really surprised me. I asked them if they would get me a bible. I couldn't believe my own voice. The

words just sort of jumped out of my mouth. Later that night I sat in my cell in deep thought on why I had asked for this bible.

I didn't know anything about the bible but for some strange reason I wanted one. The next time I saw Frank and Robert they gave me a bible and we had a good talk.

That night I prayed for the first time in my life. I prayed for Frank and Robert, and for my mom and step-dad. I prayed for forgiveness of all my sins and I asked Jesus to come into my life. After I finished praying I felt chills all over my body and I knew that Jesus had heard my prayer. I didn't change overnight but I made a big start. Any man who says he changed overnight is truly unfaithful to himself because one has a lot of habits to be broken. Over the years since I met Frank and Robert I have broken a lot of my habits. I still have several bad habits I fight with everyday but with the help of Jesus I will get through them.

By 1996 my step-dad and I were pretty close with each other. I finally realized what my he was trying to do while I was growing up and that he never hated me. In fact he loved me with all his heart. In 1996 he got real sick with cancer. I prayed all the time for him but in January 1997 he passed away. At one time I might have turned the barracks upside down in rage and frustration, but this time I didn't. For that I give thanks to Frank and Robert. My initial inspiration began with their visit to my barracks. It was this witness that helped me become the man that I am today.

This edition of ***The Lord Looseth the Prisoner*** is provided to prisoners free of charge. The continued success of this practice is dependent upon personal contributions. We are diligently working to fulfill the commission in Matthew 25:36, "*I was in prison and you visited me...*" You can be a part of this great commission by helping us provide this free gift. Will you help?

✂ ....

Yes! I will help!

Name____

Address____

Phone____

Enclosed is my contribution of $________

We will be glad to contact your friend or relative that is in prison and send a free copy of this book. Please send us their name, address and DOC #.

THE LORD LOOSETH THE PRISONER MINISTRIES, INC.
P.O. BOX 854
HEBER SPRINGS, AR 72543

(501) 362 0620

e-mail: tlltpm@arkansas.net **web address: www.tlltpm.org**

The Lord Looseth the Prisoner Ministries, Inc. is a non profit 501c3 organization and is governed by a board of directors. All contributions are tax deductible.